Doubling

Groups 2.0

By Josh Hunt

How Andy Stanley and a whole
generation of churches are
exploding with doubling groups
and the power of hospitality.

Table of Contents

Acknowledgement

Special things to the following people for helping make this a better book:

Keith Warren

Denette Hales

Mark Lott

Andy Stanley and Doubling Groups

One of the things I look forward to each fall is receiving the October edition of Outreach Magazine. This issue features two top one-hundred lists:

- Top one-hundred fastest growing churches

- Top one-hundred largest churches

It is encouraging to me because I am in so many small, struggling churches. Total attendance in these 100 churches in 2014 was 575,605. They added a combined 86,879 to their attendance compared to the previous year. That is 1671 new people attending every week—and sticking. The average annual percentage gain in attendance was 25%.

The church with the greatest numerical gain was NewSpring Church n Anderson, SC with an increase 7,736—nearly 150 new people coming and staying every single week.

But, that is not the church that really thrilled me. The one that thrilled me is one I have been following for a long time, and one that follows two principles that have been the heartbeat of my ministry for a long time. But, I am getting ahead of myself.

How is the church doing?

I attended my nephew's wedding the other day. At the rehearsal dinner, I was asked a question I have been asked many times over the years: how is the church doing these days? What are you seeing? People know that I travel a lot and they would like to get a sense of what is out there. I always answer the same way, talking about three kinds of churches.

1. **Most churches are struggling.** We know that about 80% of churches are plateaued or declining. About 4,000 churches close their doors each year.

2. **A sizeable minority are doing well. I am in a lot of these churches.** The churches where I speak tend to be above-average churches. They are healthy and growing and evangelistically vibrant—most of them. Many of them are rocking along at 5% - 10% growth per year and do so year after year. I call these churches normal churches. "Normal" in the sense that they are not doing anything a lot different from the 80% that are plateaued. They are just doing things better. The preaching is a little better. That is huge. The music is a little better—and nearly always a little younger-sounding. (Here is an insight: most of the churches that are reaching young people are using the music of young people.) Often, they are in a little better location. Location matters more than we give it credit for.

3. **There are a handful of churches that are exploding in growth**. These are the churches that make it onto the Outreach 100 each year. Andy Stanley's North Point Church in Atlanta is one such church.

How are we to respond to this last group of churches? How is it that a handful of outliers are able to explode in growth where most churches decline? If everyone was plateaued or declining, we might be tempted to believe that Jesus' words don't apply to our setting, "the harvest is plentiful." For many churches, the harvest seems anything but plentiful. But, for a handful of churches, they are bringing in an unprecedented harvest. How are we to think about these churches? I see four approaches.

1. **Many pastors ignore these churches.** This does not seem wise. In a world where we are commanded to make disciples of all nations and most churches are plateaued or declining, it does not seem wise to ignore the positive outliers. There may be many on this list that we could not learn much from because of their theology. They are either so theologically shallow, or so theologically different, that it makes learning from them a challenge. But, this would not be true of all of these churches. And, there are a lot of small and non-growing churches whose theology is suspect. Theological shallowness is not the sole domain of mega-churches. There are small churches and large churches with bad theology.

Many on the fast growing list are rock-solid theologically. #12 on the list is Houston's First Baptist Church—a church I have been to numerous times. Does anyone have any qualms with the theology of First Baptist Houston? Why aren't we all standing in line to learn from them? Some pastors do the opposite.

2. **Many slavishly follow.** Some pastors follow Saddleback in a way that Rick Warren warns will not work: they imitate every jot and tittle. There are two problems with this approach. First, any imitation and change should be done with a healthy dose of people skills and leadership skills. This is not usually the way these pastors operate. They go off to Saddleback, take notes, read the book, surround themselves with a core of yes-men and announce that things are going to change. These pastors are often unemployed. They leave behind them a bruised and bleeding church. If you talk to them, they will tell how unspiritual the people are.

There is a second reason it is not smart to slavishly follow. Your church is not in the Saddleback Valley. Your people are not from Southern California. You are not Rick Warren. We need to be like the men of Issachar—"who understood the times and knew what Israel should do." 1 Chronicles 12:32 (NIV) We need to understand the time and the place where God has called us to serve. Every place is different. Even franchises know this and adapt to their specific setting. You can often get a Green Chile burger at McDonald's in New Mexico. In Australia you can get an Aussie burger—with a beet. Yes, a red beet on a burger. Can't get that in Peoria. But, McDonald's is smart enough to adapt.

We need to be like David who, "Served God's purpose in his own generation, he fell asleep; he was buried with his fathers and his body decayed." Acts 13:36 (NIV84) Note the phrase, "in his generation." Many churches are perfectly suited to reach people in 1955.

Rick Warren says that if you follow the purpose-driven process, it won't make you like Saddleback, or any other church: "The end result in your church will look different from Saddleback and every other purpose-driven church."[1] Yet, despite Rick's warning, I have been in many churches that looked a whole lot like Saddleback.

3. **Many rail against.** It doesn't take much work to get a group of pastors talking about how the mega-churches are doing it all wrong. How different the attitude of Paul, "It is true that some preach Christ out of envy and rivalry, but others out of goodwill. The latter do so in love, knowing that I am put here for the defense of the gospel. The former preach Christ out of selfish ambition, not sincerely, supposing that they can stir up trouble for me while I am in chains. But what does it matter? The important thing is that in every way, whether from false motives or true, Christ is preached. And because of this I rejoice. Yes, and I will continue to rejoice." Philippians 1:15-18 (NIV84)

I don't hear a lot of rejoicing in some quarters. There is a lot of complaining and nit-picking. There is a lot of suspicion and scrutiny. I wonder what is driving that suspicion and scrutiny. It wouldn't be jealousy, would it?

A man who discipled me when I was in college set me straight about this kind of scrutiny and suspicion. His name was Shelby. One church we were quite critical of was W.A. Criswell's First Baptist Dallas. We could tell you a hundred reasons why Criswell had it wrong. (I don't recall any.) Shelby set me straight. "How many people have you won to Christ this week?"

---

[1] **Rick Warren,** *The Purpose Driven Church: Growth without Compromising Your Message and Mission* **(Grand Rapids, MI: Zondervan, 2007).**

"Uh, none."

"I'd say Criswell's way of doing things is better than your way of not doing things."

I often sit with pastors who complain about how awful Bill Hybels or Rick Warren or Andy Stanley is. I want to repeat Shelby's mantra, "Their way of doing things is better than your way of not doing things."

Ignoring is not good. Slavishly following is not wise. Railing against is not best. Let me show you a more excellent way.

4. **Learn from and adapt.** Learning from the top 100 is like eating fish—eat the fish and throw out the bones. I'd like to draw your attention to two things that every pastor can learn from and adapt to his ministry.

How the largest church in America grew

This year's top 100 edition was especially encouraging to me because a church that I have been following for a long time made it to the top of the list. North Point, pastored by Andy Stanley is now the largest church in America. (I am not sure what happened to Joel Osteen. His church has been at the top of the list for several years but is not on the list at all anymore.)

For years, I have been using a clip of Andy Stanley in my seminars. It works well with my emphasis on doubling groups. Andy says:

This is the most motivating thing of all for us. (This may not mean anything to you. This may be like a big, 'so-what' to you, but this is so huge to us.) We have been in groups a long time now, and as I have evaluated our history, I am convinced of this, for me and for you, if you are in a group: I believe that being in a community group that is committed to meet for a year to eighteen months and dividing and a year to eighteen months and dividing, I am convinced that if we stay in community group, and keep leading groups, that group gives Sandra and I more potential to impact more people directly and indirectly than anything else we could do together or alone, including my preaching on Sunday morning

I believe that together by being involved in a group Sandra and I have the potential to impact more people directly and indirectly in their relationship with Christ than anything else we could do together, or that I could do by myself.

Let me explain it to you this way, let me ask you some questions. The first one, you do know the answer to. How many of you plan to be alive nine years from now—you think you will make it another nine years?

Here is the question you don't have an answer to. Everybody is thinking, "I have a good nine years in me."

Here are the next two questions. First question is this: how many people do you think you can im-

pact for Christ in the next nine years? How many people? You go, "I don't know, I never thought about it."

OK, here is the next question you probably don't have an answer to: what is your plan for impacting people for Christ in the next nine years? What is your plan? "Well, if somebody comes up and says, 'How can I become a Christian I will tell them?'" Well, that is a plan! "Honk my horn and go down the neighborhood on Sunday morning and yell out, 'we are going to church!' I don't have a plan. That is a silly question. That is a preacher question. I don't have any numbers. I just try to live my life and be a good example. How about if I put a fish on the back of my car. I don't have a plan, OK?" I understand that.

Let me share something with you. Until you come up with a plan, or, until you come up with a better plan, would you just consider this plan? This plan is simple. You don't have to sing, dance, learn to play the guitar, speak in public, juggle. . . you don't have to learn anything new. If you will simply get in a community group and allow God to do what he wants to do in you and through you and at the end of a year or eighteen months, start a new group, and do that for another year or eighteen months and start a new group, did you know that in nine years you would have impacted directly or indirectly over six hundred and forty people?

Now, if you have a better nine-year plan, run your plan, share it with me, we will spend a weekend talking about it, but until you come up with plan, why not do this? Simply by being in the system you would have impacted six hundred and forty people. Just by being a part of the system—you have to do something, right?

And these are not just fictitious numbers to me because I have been doing this for over nine years. And as Sandra and I look at the leaders in groups and the hundreds of people that are in groups as a result of our first group, this is a reality to us.

Now, let me tell you something that will really blow your mind. If we could ever get our arms around this, we could make history together. You ready for this? Because of the number of people in our organization on all of our campuses that are already in small groups—just adults, not children, not college students, not high school students—if you just took the number of adults that we currently have in groups, if, over the next nine years we just continue to do groups the way I have explained it, at the end of nine years we would have over half a million people in groups. [2]

I will never forget the night I first heard Andy say this. I was driving in south Texas from Houston to Beaumont. It was late at night. I was listening to the Go Fish sermon series. I heard the clip above and thought, "I have never heard a pastor say this. I have never heard a pastor stand before his church and say (essentially), 'I am in a group that is doubling; I want you to be in a group that is doubling.'"

---

[2] Andy Stanley, *Go Fish* DVD.

Andy Stanley is not the only next generation leader who champions the idea of doubling groups. Neil Cole has written extensively on this:

> *In his book,* Disciples Are Made Not Born, *Walter Henrichsen described a display at the Museum of Science and Industry in Chicago which featured a checkerboard with 1 grain of rice on the first square, 2 on the second, 4 on the third, then 8, 16, 32, 64, 128 etc. Somewhere down the board, there was so much rice that it was spilling over into neighboring squares—so the display ended there. Above the demonstration was a question: At this rate of doubling each square, how much rice would you have on the checkerboard by the time you reached the 64th square? To find the answer to this riddle, you punched a button on the console in front of you, and the answer flashed on a screen above the board: Enough to cover the entire subcontinent of India, 50 feet deep!13 There would be 153 billion tons of rice—more than the world rice harvest for the next 1000 years.*
>
> *You may have heard the fable of a father who offered his two sons a choice of either one dollar a week for 52 weeks, or one cent the first week, and then the amount doubled the next week to just 2 cents and, continuing for 52 weeks. One son took the buck; the other took a chance and accepted the penny. We all know who wins: the son who took the dollar would have 52 dollars at the end of the year. The one who began with a penny would have by the end of the year, enough money to*

pay off the national debt, and still have plenty left over for himself!16 That's a father with some deep pockets!

Imagine a water lily growing on a pond with a surface of 14,000 square feet. The leaf of this species of water lily has a surface of 15.5 square inches. At the beginning of the year the water lily has exactly one leaf. After one week there are two leaves. A week later, four. After sixteen weeks half of the water surface is covered with leaves.17 The authors then ask, "How long will it take until the second half of the pond will also be covered? Another sixteen weeks? No. It will take just a single week and the pond will be completely covered."[3]

I worked out the math based on what Andy said. A group of ten that doubles every eighteen months will reach a thousand people for God in ten years. Why isn't it happening everywhere? That is the subject of the next chapter.

---

[3] *Cultivating A Life For God* by Neil Cole

Speed of the Leader;
Speed of the Team

Doubling groups are working at North Point because Andy Stanley regularly stands before his church and says, "I am in a group that is doubling; I want you to be in a group that is doubling." He didn't just say it just once. He says it every year. Here is another example.

> So because of our leadership here, and because of Bill Willits and his team, we have found ways to give people an opportunity to be in a closed, predictable group for a year to eighteen months and then to divide and start new groups.

> Sandra and I are in our twelfth group. We started doing this before Northpoint was started. It has been an incredible, incredible experience. In fact, I will tell you a story. Our group is about to divide. We have been together for a year and a half, so it is time to divide. So, we have that awful, awkward conversation that every group has to have. How are we going to divide? Who is going with who? Who is keeping who? It is always very, very awkward. Breaking up is hard to do.

Why isn't it happening everywhere? Because Andy is the only pastor I have ever heard say, "I am in a group that doubles; I want you to be in a group that doubles." I believe this is something that every church could learn from. You might not want to do everything like Northpoint. Could you prayerfully consider doing this one thing: stand before your people and say, "I am in a group that is committed to doubling. I want you to be in a group that is committing to doubling." Andy spells this out in his excellent book, *Creating Community: Five Keys to Building a Small Group Culture:*

> *Whenever I talk to senior pastors about their small-group ministries, I always ask about their personal small-group experience. The majority of the time—and I mean the vast majority of the time—it turns out that the pastor is not actively participating in a group. At that point I say something rude. I think it is hypocritical for a pastor to champion something he isn't willing to participate in himself. Meanwhile, the small-groups director is standing there giving me imaginary high fives. He or she knows what many senior pastors don't: Groups don't really impact a local church until they become part of a church's culture. And that begins with senior leadership.[4]*

Bill Hybels says, "The leader must embody the vision." Growing groups is not the only way to grow a church. But, if you are going to grow your church through growing groups, the leader must embody the vision.

---

[4] *Creating Community: Five Keys to Building a Small Group Culture* by Andy Stanley, Bill Willits

I have a friend, Lance Witt, who used to be the Small Group Pastor at Rick Warren's Saddleback Church until he moved into the Executive Pastor role. He told me that when Rick got in a group, group life skyrocketed. But just as important as Rick getting in a group was that Rick began to talk about his group in his messages. By doing so, he raised the value of group life and it began to get into the DNA of the church life at Saddleback. People began to think, "If it's important for someone as busy as Rick Warren, maybe it should be important for me." As the leader embodies the vision of small groups, the people get it. In contrast, here is what most pastors say, at least by their actions: "I am not in a group, but I think you should be in one."

Johnny Hunt is another example of a pastor that leads by example. In a world where many pundits are claiming the day of the Sunday School is over, he has seen his Sunday School grow from 600 to nearly 5,000. His Minister of Education has written a couple of great books on group life including *Sunday School in HD*. Johnny Hunt's example and cheerleading are a real key. He spoke at my home church a few years ago and I heard him share about how he personally attends a Sunday School class every week. He has plenty of responsibilities that could provide an adequate excuse—including serving as the President of the Southern Baptist Convention. Still, he takes time to attend a group each week. His Minister of Education, Allan Taylor speaks of the importance of this: "How can the pastor champion the cause of Sunday School? I think it starts by joining and attending a Sunday School class himself. His example will send an unequivocal message to the entire congregation that Sunday School is important around here."[5]

Pastor Larry Osborn champions sermon-based groups in this excellent book, *Sticky Church*. Groups are encouraged to get together and talk about the pastor. You might be thinking, "They do that at my church already!" In this case, what they mean is they encourage people to talk about how to apply the pastor's sermons to their lives. While the idea of sermon-based groups is a good one, I don't think you can attribute their success to sermon-based groups. Larry Osborne leads North Coast Church in Vista, CA. He is a pioneer in the multi-site movement, and as such, has led his church to have twenty weekend services with 7,000 attending. Much of the credit must go to Larry Osborn's leading by example, not to the specific strategy of sermon-based groups. In an Outreach magazine article, he says, "Involve all key leaders. Our lay leadership and staff are expected to be in a Growth Group. If your key leaders are too busy to be in a small group, it sends the message that small groups are an extra-credit offering for those with time on their hands.[6]

Wayne Cordeiro another top-100 pastor that believes in leading by example. He warns pastors, "Your church will be no more involved than you are involved. She will be no

[5] Alan Taylor, *Sunday School in HD*. p. 134
[6] Outreach Magazine, Special Issue, 2008, page 86.

more devoted than you are. No more genuine than you are. No more positive than you are."[7]

Nelson Searcy is the pastor of The Journey in New York City. He believes in semester-by-semester groups. He has an excellent book on the subject called *Activate*. They have more people attending groups than they have attending worship. But, I don't think the success can be attributed to the semester-by-semester approach so much as the success can be attributed to the pastor and staff leading by example. His words: "Most leader pastors share a common temptation when it comes to small groups: They want to turn the operation over to someone else. They want to give it to a dedicated staff specialist so they don't have to deal with it. We know! In theory this doesn't sound like a bad idea. But the truth is, handing the system off too early is the worst thing a pastor can do for the small group system. As a matter of fact, when it comes to implementing a successful small group system, **every single person has to be involved, starting with the top.**"[8]

Pastor, if you would lead your groups to grow, get in a group. Do what Bill Hybels says, "The leader must embody the vision." He expands on this:

---

[7] *The Irresistible Church: 12 Traits of a Church Heaven Applauds* by Wayne Cordeiro

[8] Nelson Searcy, *Activate*. Kindle edition.

Leaders must never expect from others anything more than they're willing to deliver themselves. They should never expect higher levels of commitment, creativity, persistence, or patience than what they themselves manifest on a regular basis.

If you cannot say, "Follow me," to your followers—and mean it—then you've got a problem. A big one. Speed of the leader, speed of the team.[9]

I close this chapter with one more example of a leader who understood we must lead by example, the Apostle Paul. He said, "Follow my example, as I follow the example of Christ." 1 Corinthians 11:1 (NIV)

My prayer is that God would raise up a whole generation of pastors who say, "Follow me, as I live out 2 Timothy 2.2, "And the things you have heard me say in the presence of many witnesses entrust to reliable people who will also be qualified to teach others."

[9] Bill Hybels, *Axiom: Powerful Leadership Proverbs* (Grand Rapids, MI: Zondervan, 2008).

Hospitality

I can summarize my life message in one sentence: you can double a group in two years or less by inviting every member and every prospect to every fellowship every month.

A longer, one-paragraph version goes like this: A group of ten that doubles every eighteen months can reach a thousand people for God in ten years. One of the best ways of growing a group is through relationships. The gospel spreads best on the bridges of existing relationships. Donald McGavran called these *The Bridges of God.* Hospitality makes relational evangelism intentional evangelism. If we love them they will come and they will come to love our Lord. It is not enough to tell them about a God who loves them, we must love them. It is not enough to tell them the words about grace, we must be gracious to them.

Do the top 100 have anything to say about hospitality? Once again, let me quote the pastor of the nation's largest church:

> *When I got out of Seminary I started working with High School students I learned two things real quick, number one. I learned it was possible to*

*create environments where unchurched, unbeliev-
ing kids could come and even though they didn't
believe what we believe they would come back
the next week to hear more. And I also learned a
more important thing. I learned that if you can get
unchurched, unbelieving people in a community
of believers that are loving each other and caring
for each other and being real Christians, that being
in that community breaks down the barriers to
unbelief. It strips away big objections—good God
and bad things happening to good people and
all those legitimate questions. You get somebody
in the community where the church is being the
church and somehow the edges get softer and
people's hearts open up and life change happens. And so, we started creating environments
where kids started coming and lives started being
changed and do you know where we got the resis-
tance? From the church people! And so one night
I am sitting in this meeting. It had been going an
hour and a half because we had a band and video
and stuff and there are all these wonderful church
people. . . I know many of them, knew many of
them for many years, some of them come here
now. And the meeting was, "Andy, if you keep doing this, creating these environments, here is what
is going to happen, and all the potential horrible
stuff and sex drugs and rock and roll and whoa! It's
going to be terrible.*

*And I just kept thinking, "Where is this coming
from?" Toward the end of the meeting a lady stood
up toward my right. She is still a friend of mine. She
stood up, tears in her eyes, her voice quivering, and
she said, "I am amazed at what I have heard. For*

an hour I have listened to everyone talk about how afraid they are about what might happen. Can I tell you what has happened? My two sons, who have never been involved in a church look forward to every Wednesday night and never miss. And, it you shut down this program, I am afraid they will never step foot inside a church again." She sat down.

And I made up my mind. I am going to spend the rest of my life finding people who understand that you can create environments in a local church that allow us to partner with people who are fishing. And I want to create environments for people and as they come and as they get involved in a community of believers their belief system begins to change, not because we have confronted, not because we give them specific answers to specific questions, although there is a time and a place of that. But, because they are in the presence, as much as they'll ever be in the presence of the living savior.

The nation's largest church is only nineteen years old. It was able to grow so rapidly (in part) because the pastor, Andy Stanley regularly stands before the people and says, "I am in a group that is doubling; I want you to be in a group that is doubling."

They grow by creating environments where unchurched people can kick tires in an atmosphere of grace and acceptance. They have discovered that if they will love people, people's hearts will warm up to a message about a

God who loves them. They have discovered that if they are gracious to people, people's hearts warm up to a message about grace. If they will befriend people, people will warm up to a message about, "What a friend we have in Jesus."

North Point has grown by loving people in common, ordinary, pedestrian ways. But, they are not the only church that does. Barna's reserach shows that this is common in this next generation of churches, "We hear again and again, both from the unchurched and from local churches that are deeply engaged with the unchurched in their communities, that loving, genuine relationships are the only remaining currency readily exchanged between the churched and the churchless."[10]

And, when it comes to developing relationships, there are few better ways than a party

> *John Chandler, who leads a Christian community in Austin, Texas, shared this: We've by far had the most success inviting people into our community life by inviting them to serve alongside us. As a matter of fact, that's about the only thing that's worked consistently as far as "official" church activities go. The other thing that has worked is parties—birthday parties, Super Bowl parties—where*

---

[10] *Churchless: Understanding Today's Unchurched and How to Connect with Them* by George Barna, David Kinnaman

we invite churched friends and unchurched friends just to connect.[11]

Willow Creek and Matthew Parties

North Point is not the only top-100 churches that uses hospitality to reach people. Willow Creek uses hospitality as well. Bill Hybels calls them Matthew Parties. They are based on Jesus' encounter with Matthew (also known as Levi). Here is the story from Luke 5.

> *After this, Jesus went out and saw a tax collector by the name of Levi sitting at his tax booth. "Follow me," Jesus said to him, and Levi got up, left everything and followed him. Then Levi held a great banquet for Jesus at his house, and a large crowd of tax collectors and others were eating with them. But the Pharisees and the teachers of the law who belonged to their sect complained to his disciples, "Why do you eat and drink with tax collectors and sinners?" Jesus answered them, "It is not the healthy who need a doctor, but the sick. I have not come to call the righteous, but sinners to repentance." Luke 5:27–32 (NIV)*

Based on this example Bill Hybels and the people of Willow Creek use Matthew parties to build bridges to people who are far from God.

---

11 Ibid, Kindle location 472

Willow Creek wrote a drama that I have used many times to communicate the value of hospitality. (If you would like to teach on the value of hospitality in your church, I strongly recommend you use this video. <u>Available on Willow Creek's</u> <u>website.)</u> It features a character named Evan Powell who is the quintessential "Unchurched Harry." He meets a woman he is interested in and she invites him to church. Not interested.

She invites him to a home group Bible Study. Not interested.

People from the Bible study invite him to go bowling. Not interested.

They invite him to dinner. Not interested.

They invite him to a music festival. Not interested.

They invite him to a vintage car show. Bingo. Evan can't resist. He loves vintage cars. He goes to the vintage car show and discovers one of the guys in the group has two vintage cars. This guy invites him over to see the cars and a friendship develops. The friendship opens the door for Evan to become a friend of Jesus. Everything changes when we love people rather than just telling them about Christ's love.

Here is a typical Matthew Party in Hybels' own words:

Back in the early days of Willow, we talked with such frequency about the "Matthew Party" story in Luke 5 that it became part of the fabric of our church culture. Operating with Matthew's intuition for discerning next steps in the lives of seekers became sort of a way of life, and lots of us started throwing Matthew Parties, for want of a better name. They weren't part of a formal, programmatic effort. They were just casual ways to help people who were outside the family of God to get inside the family of God. Willow folks would grab a few people from the office and a few people from church and host a backyard barbeque or a pool party or hang out shooting pool in someone's basement. During the eighties and nineties, we heard of scores of people coming to faith as a result of these parties.

Over time, my desire to reflect Matthew's remarkable courage kept increasing. I got addicted to sticking my neck out there just as he did, pulling believers and nonbelievers into the same room and trusting God with the results. After a while, although the larger-scale buzz at Willow died down, I was one of those eternal optimists who never stopped believing in the power of the party. I never stopped seeking ways to gather some new-life friends together with some old-life friends just to see what might transpire. I never stopped rejoicing over that particular work of the Holy Spirit in my life, who used the simplicity of throwing a party to craft me into the type of person who better reflects the heart of the Father.

At Christmastime last year, I did what I have done every year following Willow's Christmas Eve service: I threw a Matthew Party. Despite wall-to-wall meetings, planning sessions, and run-throughs that week, my mind kept drifting to the Matthew Party that was only days away. I couldn't wait!

I had invited about twenty people who were living extremely far from God, by their own admission. These men and women had never been to Willow before, had never been to my house before, and spiritually speaking would profess to be "going it alone."

To that group, I added about twenty people who were in the Seeker Slow Lane — the remedial class of Christianity, you might say. On the rare occasion when I would badger them mercilessly, they'd agree to come to Willow. But it was sporadic attendance at best, usually involving a fair amount of kicking and screaming on their part. Most of them had been to my house previously to attend other parties, and all of them knew I was "working" on them, nudging them along the (very) slow path to God. Maybe they would step across the line of faith someday, but in my estimation, it was going to take some time. A lot of time.

In addition to the twenty or so people who were very far from God, and the twenty or so people who were in-progress types, I had sprinkled in a dozen or so very strong Christ-followers from Willow to mix it up a bit. The screening process for this group in particular had been intense! I knew I couldn't afford any overzealous types showing up. No truth vigilantes. No bounty hunters. Just normal, mature, relationally intelligent, open-hearted, radically inclusive people who understood how high the stakes were that night — after all, I was going to put them in a room with friends of mine who, apart from a bona fide miracle, would spend eternity apart from God.

As with every other year, fifteen minutes before guests arrived, my heart started beating fast. I'm sure the tension I felt was completely natural — I had no way to control the outcome of the party, no way of knowing how the guests would interact, and no way to prepare for the exact conversations that would unfold and what God would choose to do as a result.

But I wouldn't have traded that anxiety for anything in the world! As I greeted the first guests to arrive, I braced for the adventure to come as a final burst of adrenaline exploded. Here we go!

I wish you could have been there to watch what unfolded that night. In my house in Barrington, Illinois, in the twenty-first century, we enjoyed an approximation of Matthew's first-century experience. It was incredible to witness so many God-moments in the making, not to mention it was just a heck of a party. The first time I glanced down at my watch, it was well past midnight, and guests ended up staying until two o'clock the next morning — and only left then because I kicked them out.

So what was it that gave it the buzz? What made it such a magical, edgy experience? I mulled over questions like those in the hours and days that followed. Want to know what I decided? The single greatest reason that the party was such a success was because the Christ-followers I'd invited from Willow did exactly what Christ wants all of his followers to do: they took a walk across the room.

When the Willow people had first arrived, they gathered in little Creeker circles, safely huddling together to talk about the weather, the Christmas Eve stage set, plans for the weekend, you name it. (They had to start somewhere, I guess.) But then, after about twenty minutes, it happened — and I was so proud of them when it did. One by one, they looked around the room and started excusing themselves from each other's company. "Well, I'm not going to stay in this circle all night," they would murmur as their minds raced. I'm going to walk across the living room and stick out my hand and introduce myself to someone.

"Excuse me," they would say, with a complete lack of confidence. And then slowly they turned and walked. And how I related to the thoughts they had as they made those walks. I'd made hundreds of similar walks across rooms, and I knew how fast their hearts were beating, how dry their mouths were becoming, how curious they were about what would take place once they said, "Hi. My name is …"

Every step of the way across my living room that night, each Christ-follower was thinking, I have no idea how this is going to turn out. I don't know if this guy is going to want to talk to me. I don't know if that woman will want to engage in conversation with me. But you know what? I'm going to give it a shot. I'm going to pray every step of the way as I walk across this room, I'm going to introduce myself, and then I'm going to step back and just see if God does anything more.

The discussions instantly began to light up. I was so grateful that the Spirit was opening doors! Everyone at the party had attended the Christmas Eve service together, and that shared experience provided the perfect conversational springboard. Some people talked about how they'd never been on the inside of a church before. (What an honor that Willow was their first experience!) Others admitted to just needing "more facts," and still others had recently purchased Rick Warren's book The Purpose Driven Life, intending to read it over the holidays.

As I meandered through the crowd that night, I thought about all of the requests I'd made of God in the days leading up to the party. "Oh, if this person and that person could get together and be in conversation with one another, that would be incredible!" Or "If only so-and-so and my other friend could chat, that would be so kinetic — they have so much in common." Sure enough, while I wandered around my own home that night, refilling drinks and making sure people had enough to eat, I would catch a glimpse of those exact pairings occurring. "God is good!" I whispered quietly. "God is so good!"

Thankfully, no Pharisee types showed up at my house that night to throw water on the delicate sparks that were flickering. I remember walking back into the kitchen with a feeling of soul-level satisfaction. It took hours before that buzz wore off! Finally, after I had given everyone the boot, I halfheartedly picked up the remaining dishes, grabbed stray glasses, and headed back into the kitchen, dazed by the significance of all that had happened.

Sometime just before daybreak, my mind still racing from the mystical aspects of the party, I thought to myself, the whole thing comes down to nights just like this one. The future of the kingdom of God comes down to whether individual rank-and-file Christ-followers will do in their everyday lives what just happened in my home tonight!

It really is true: the spread of the gospel — at least in today's reality — boils down to whether you and I will continue to seek creative ways to engage our friends, inviting them to explore the abundance of the Christ-following life and helping them choose eternity with God instead of settling for a terrible fate when this life is all said and done.[12]

---

[12] Bill Hybels, *Just Walk across the Room: Simple Steps Pointing People to Faith* (Grand Rapids, MI: Zondervan, 2008).

Rick Warren has done a similar thing. His words:

> *For years, Kay and I would host an informal coffee in our home on the fourth Sunday night of each month. Called the "Pastor's Chat," it was simply an opportunity for new members and visitors from the previous month to meet us face-to-face and ask any questions they had. We'd place a sign-up sheet out on the patio before Sunday services and the first thirty to sign up would get to come. The chats would last from 7 to 10 p.m. This simple act of hospitality brought in hundreds of new members and established many relationships that Kay and I cherish today. Hospitality grows a healthy church.*[13]

Rick Warren's Small Group Pastor, Steve Gladen teaches all of their small groups to use parties as a means of reaching people:

> *Follow his example and host a neighborhood picnic or barbecue. Plan to go to a lake or park and have everybody in your group invite a friend. Or have a Super Bowl party. Relax and have fun. The sole purpose of this social event is for your small group to get together with seekers and build relationships. But don't expect lost people to act like anything but lost people. That's one of the huge mistakes we make. We start with this sort of*

---

[13] Rick Warren, *The Purpose Driven Church: Growth without Compromising Your Message and Mission* (Grand Rapids, MI: Zondervan, 2007).

judgment and condemnation rather than just say-
ing, "Man, we're so glad you're here. Come on in."
Just remember that they need Jesus. This is your
chance to show them the love of Christ. Just accept
them.[14]

Doubling groups and hospitality are two tools of top-100 churches. There is one more thing we must do to see a doubling group movement.

---

[14] Steve Gladen, *Leading Small Groups with Purpose: Everything You Need to Lead a Healthy Group* (Grand Rapids, MI: Baker, 2012).

How I Solved the
Worker Shortage

What did Jesus say would be the bottleneck of the evangelistic, disciple-making process?

Would we fail because of lack of programs or money or ideas or literature? No. Jesus did tell us what the bottleneck would be, and it would not be any of those things.

Jesus said the harvest is plentiful but the workers are few. Workers have always been the bottleneck to the evangelistic, disciple-making process.

The next thing He said was, "Pray." The next thing He did was to say, "Go, I am sending you out." Pray and send.

People are always surprised by this. I have been in several top 100 churches. I was in a church recently where the pastor asked me to speak to the staff. "How many will I be speaking to?" "About 60." There are a lot of churches in America that don't have sixty in attendance. This church had 60+ on the payroll.

There is a tendency to think of those top-100 churches and think, "Man if we had that number of workers, we could really do something for God." Do you know what they are thinking about in top-100 churches? "We can't get enough workers. Do you have any idea how many workers you need to run a church of this size?"

How I solved the worker shortage

When I was on church staff we prayed about workers every week in staff meeting. I believe every staff would do well to gather each week and pray to the Lord of the harvest to raise up workers. I did one more thing. Once I did this, I never struggled to find adult workers again.

Our old way of doing things required that we recruit people with the gift of teaching to lead groups. Barna says 9% of those he has surveyed have the gift of teaching.[15] This is a problem because my average group size was about ten. This means I needed to recruit nearly all of those with the gift of teaching into the teaching ministry. Some were not willing to serve. We were always struggling to find workers. What if I could employ people with other spiritual gifts—gifts like leadership and encouragement—to lead small groups?

My style of teaching has always heavily reliant on the question and answer approach. My preparation consisted of coming up with about twenty questions that I would

[15] https://www.barna.org/barna-update/faith-spirituality/211-survey-describes-the-spiritual-gifts-that-christians-say-they-have

use in class. In addition to the questions, I would have some background material from commentators, as most teachers do. But, the flow of the lesson centered on my list of twenty questions.

I would always know the answers to these questions. Bible study is not about "pooled ignorance."

By the way, I am tired of hearing people say, "We don't really need teachers; we just need facilitators." I don't want facilitators. I want teachers. Jesus said to go into all the world and teach all nations. He didn't say to facilitate discussions in all nations. He said to teach.

Wikipedia defines a facilitator this way:

> *A facilitator is someone who helps a group of people understand their common objectives and assists them to plan how to achieve these objectives; in doing so, the facilitator remains "neutral" meaning he/she does not take a particular position in the discussion.[16]*

Does not have a particular position in the discussion? Really? That is not the kind of group leader I want. I want them to have more than positions, I want them to have convictions. I want them to teach using questions, as Jesus did. But, I want them to have convictions about what they

---

[16] http://en.wikipedia.org/wiki/Facilitator

are discussing. (For more on Jesus' teaching, see my book, *Teach Like Jesus.*)

I took a group and saw it grow from less than ten to about thirty. I made several appeals for workers to take part of the group, but didn't have any takers. One day, a man who had turned down my request to lead a group was sitting next to me as I taught.

He had actually taught before and enjoyed teaching. What he hated was the preparation. He would tend to put if off all week and then get up really early on Sunday morning to prepare. He said it ruined his Sundays.

This day, he would watch me teach in an up-close-and-personal way. He watched as I asked question #1, allowed the group to discuss, and moved to question #2… on through the list of questions.

In the real world, it is not just a matter of asking twenty questions. Group life is messy. The group will get you off the list. Some questions don't work and sometimes the conversation will naturally cause you to jump ahead. Still, it gave my friend an idea.

After group was over, my friend made me an offer, "If you will keep writing these questions that you write for yourself, and get them to me a week ahead of time, I will take a group." Done.

Soon others in the church wanted my notes. Once I started making these <u>Good Questions</u> available, I never struggled to find adult workers again. The reason is fairly simple. It is just math. In the old system, I was looking for people with the gift of teaching and had to recruit pretty much all of them to satisfy demand. Now, I could recruit people with gifts of leadership and encouragement who could lead groups. Many of these people actually made better group leaders than people with the true gift of teaching. People with gift of teaching tended to want to lecture and think that was teaching.

I told others about Good Questions and started mailing them out. It was the beginning of a little cottage industry. But, this distribution system was just too cumbersome. By the time I printed, folded and stamped the lessons . . . it was all just too much trouble.

Then came the Internet. As soon as I discovered the Internet, I realized I had a distribution system. I put together a web page and started distributing my Good Questions online. I gradually refined them into the form they are now in.

A few years back I had a really big innovation. I decided to provide answers to the questions.

Prior to this I had operated on the assumption that there were plenty of good books and commentaries that contained the answers. It occurred to me that the people who used my lessons didn't have the theological library that I had. And, even if they did, they really didn't like digging and researching all that much. Remember, these were people with gifts in leadership and encouragement, not teaching.

About this time, the digital revolution was in full swing. I had a growing WordSearch library. I bought my first Kindle and began replacing many of my paper books with Kindle books. I bought Logos Bible Software and started building my library in it.

I am still building my library. Today, I wrote a thanksgiving lesson based on Luke 17.11ff—the story of the nine ungrateful lepers. I added two books to my Logos library to provide material for this lesson.

Logos is set up so that if Luke 17.11 is mentioned in any of my books, I will find it. If Max Lucado ever mentioned Luke 17.11, I will find it and provide it to my group leaders. If Charles Swindoll or John MacArthur or Charles Stanley ever mentioned Luke 17.11, I will find it. I will find the same material good preachers and communicators use and put material into the hands of group leaders. I want to make group leaders sound brilliant. And, I want to help Small Group Pastors to find workers.

Back to the main point: once I started providing question-based curriculum, I never struggled to find group leaders again.

Conclusion

We can take our world for God by giving the ministry to laymen who are using their gifts to grow their groups, to double their groups every two years or less. A group of ten that doubles every eighteen months will reach a thousand people in ten years. It is happening. It is happening like never before.

Bill Hybels spoke at North Point's fifteen-year anniversary. He described North Point by saying it is the fastest movement in history. How did they do it? Doubling groups that are growing through hospitality are two key components. They are two components every church can use to reach their community.

May God richly bless your efforts to reach people for Him. We must work in the power of the Holy Spirit. We must work in faith. We must work in humility. May God richly bless His work through His people for His glory.

Bonus: Sample Lesson
Awake, Lesson #1
Good Questions Have Small Groups Talking
www.joshhunt.com

Jonah 1.1 – 3; 3.1 – 5, 10

OPEN

Let's each share your name and when was the last time you were on a boat?

DIG

1. What do you know about Jonah? Who was Jonah?

Jonah was a prophet; he was not a priest. Priests served in the Temple. They offered sacrifices. They led worship. A prophet was different. A prophet was a reformer. A prophet was an activist —kind of a gadfly, kind of a troublemaker. Prophets were always pricking people's consciences. Israel always had a lot of priests but generally just one prophet at a time because that was all Israel could stand.

One day the word of the Lord comes to this prophet Jonah. When you hear from God, and sometimes you will, it may be only a few words, but they can change your life. — John Ortberg, *All the Places You'll Go . . . except When You Don't: God Has Placed before You an Open Door. What Will You Do?* (Carol Stream, IL: Tyndale, 2015).

2. How did Jonah respond to God's call?

Life isn't easy when you're a prophet. The word of the Lord comes to Jonah:

> Could you, would you go to preach?
> Could you, would you go to reach
> The people in Assyria?
> For you fit my criteria.

> And Jonah says to the Lord:

> I would not go there in a boat.
> I would not go there in a float.

> I would not go there in a gale.
> I would not go there in a whale.

> I do not like the people there.
> If they all died, I would not care.

> I will not go to that great town.
> I'd rather choke. I'd rather drown.

> I will not go by land or sea.
> So stop this talk and let me be.

John Ortberg, *All the Places You'll Go . . . except When You Don't: God Has Placed before You an Open Door. What Will You Do?* (Carol Stream, IL: Tyndale, 2015).

3. Why wouldn't Jonah respond to God's call?

Jonah was a prophet, but he was a prophet to Israel. He had nothing to do with other countries. They didn't have Scripture. They didn't have a Temple. They didn't know about sacrifices. They didn't know God. Word comes to him, "Go to Nineveh and preach." It's striking how this is expressed. Not "Go to Nineveh and preach to it"; "Go to Nineveh and preach against it," the text says. That's a daunting task.

Nineveh was the capital of Assyria. In the seventh and eighth centuries BC, Assyria was the great world power. It chewed up and spit out countries right and left. It would put the populations of countries that it defeated on death marches. It practiced genocide as state policy. When Israel was split into two sections, there was the northern kingdom of ten tribes and the southern kingdom of just two tribes. The northern kingdom was captured and basically vaporized, basically obliterated, by Assyria.

Nineveh was hated so much that the prophet Nahum named it "the city of blood." That's what it was called. That was its title. "Woe to the city of blood, full of lies, full of plunder, never without victims! . . . Piles of dead." Now you think about this: "Bodies without number, people stumbling over the corpses" (Nahum 3:1, 3).

Nahum predicts the fall of Nineveh: "Your wound is fatal. All who hear the news about you clap their hands at your fall, for who has not felt your endless cruelty?" (Nahum 3:19). Nineveh is so hated, not just for cruelty, but for endless cruelty. When it is destroyed, Nahum says, people are going to clap. They are going to stand up and cheer.

Nahum said very strong, condemning words about Nineveh, but where do you think Nahum was when he said those words?

He was in Israel. — John Ortberg, *All the Places You'll Go . . . except When You Don't: God Has Placed before You an Open Door. What Will You Do?* (Carol Stream, IL: Tyndale, 2015).

4. What do we learn about God's calling on our lives from Jonah's story?

What we do know is that God had opened a door for Jonah, and Jonah not only didn't go through it but ran the other way, and the implication is that he did this because he was afraid. "I'm very brave generally, only today I happen to have a headache," said Tweedledum in Lewis Carroll's Through the Looking Glass.[50]

God said to Jonah, "I have set before you an open door. It leads to Nineveh. Jonah would have gone, but he had a headache.

Sometimes open doors are not fun. Sometimes they're not even safe. Always they're about something greater than our own benefit. Often they lead to Nineveh.

Nineveh is the place God calls you where you do not want to go. Nineveh is trouble. Nineveh is danger. Nineveh is fear. What do you do when God says to you, "Go to Nineveh; go to the place you do not want to go"? Because God will say that to you.

Now Jonah arises in response to the word of the Lord. He does leave home, but not for Nineveh. He heads for Tarshish.

It may happen like this: I know God is asking me to go to Nineveh. I know God wants me to confront this person, have a conversation about the truth, but that would be hard. That would be unpleasant. I don't want to face that pain, so I'll just go to Tarshish.

I know God is calling me to serve in this area, but I don't want to. It might be humbling. It might be difficult. It might be scary. I don't want to do that, so I'll run away to Tarshish.

I know God has called me to teach or counsel or build or lead or invite or give, but I might fail. It might be hard. I might be anxious. So I'll get on a ship bound for Tarshish.

But here's what matters: fear is never overcome by situation avoidance. We were born to be brave. The consistent command to us is the command that came to a fearful leader named Joshua: "Be strong and courageous . . . for the LORD your God will be with you" (Joshua 1:9). Three times in the first chapter of the book of Jonah we're told that Jonah runs —not just from his calling but "from the presence of the LORD" (1:3, NRSV). Yet the antidote to fear is the presence of God. — John Ortberg, *All the Places You'll Go . . . except When You Don't: God Has Placed before You an Open Door. What Will You Do?* (Carol Stream, IL: Tyndale, 2015).

5. Have you ever run from God's calling? How so?

When I was in seventh grade, there was a girl in our class I'll call Shirley. She was awkward; she wore the wrong clothes. She had red hair and freckles and buckteeth. No one sat next to her at lunch; no one invited her to be on their team.

I could have done those things. I could have been her friend. Or I could have at least gone out of my way to be kind to her. But I didn't. I suppose I was afraid that if I did, I might have been as rejected as she was. I wasn't the most popular kid in the class, but I wasn't as lowly as Shirley, and I wasn't willing to give up what status I had to befriend her.

I was running to Tarshish. — John Ortberg, *All the Places You'll Go . . . except When You Don't: God Has Placed before You an Open Door. What Will You Do?* (Carol Stream, IL: Tyndale, 2015).

6. Locate Tarshish and Nineveh on a map. Did Jonah run in the general direction of God's call?

Tarshish is significant, not just because it's in the opposite direction from Nineveh, but because in many ways it was the opposite kind of city.

Nineveh was a military city. Tarshish was not a military power, but it had great wealth. It was a pioneer in trade. Commerce over the sea was kind of like new technology and was making some people rich. Not a bad thing necessarily, but it has a way of leading to greed and arrogance and pride. So that phrase —"a ship of Tarshish" —became a symbol of wealth in the ancient world.

It actually comes up a number of times in the Old Testament. Isaiah says, "The LORD of hosts has a day against all that is proud and lofty, against all that is lifted up and high; . . . against all the ships of Tarshish. . . . The haughtiness of people shall be humbled" (Isaiah 2:12, 16-17, NRSV).

A similar image is used in Ezekiel: "The ships of Tarshish serve as carriers for your wares. . . . With your great wealth and your wares you enriched the kings of the earth. Now you are shattered by the sea" (Ezekiel 27:25, 33-34).

The ships of Tarshish became symbols of wealth and self-sufficiency and power and greed. Is it hard to imagine that once a group of human beings was so deluded that they thought technology, wealth, and a clever economic system could make them secure?

Jonah ran away to Wall Street. Jonah ran away to Madison Avenue. Jonah ran away to Silicon Valley. Jonah gets on the ship of Tarshish. People have been headed for that ship for a long time. Jonah thinks he's running toward safety, but maybe what really looks safe from a human perspective is not actually safe at all. Maybe the only safe place is to be in the will of God for your life, even if it means choosing the door to Nineveh, that scary place you don't want to go. — John Ortberg, *All the Places You'll Go . . . except When You Don't: God Has Placed before You an Open Door. What Will You Do?* (Carol Stream, IL: Tyndale, 2015).

7. Have you ever responded to God's call? What was that like? Who has a story?

Sometimes I'm running away from Nineveh, and a door opens up on a ship of Tarshish. Sometimes I fail to go through open doors because I don't recognize their presence.

Chuck Colson is disgraced and sent to prison, and he finds doors opening to ministry there that never opened to him in the White House. Helen Keller faces severe disabilities, yet a door is opened to her precisely because of them to help untold millions. A Sunday school teacher named Rosa Parks is told to sit in the back of a bus, and her quiet refusal opens the door to the conscience of a nation.

A woman at our church said to an eight-year-old boy who was all dressed up on Easter morning, "You look so handsome. Did you get that outfit for Easter?"

No, the little fellow explained. He got it for the funeral of his daddy, who had just died a few weeks ago.

It turns out that this woman also lost her father when she was eight years old. She got down on her knees, took him in her arms, and spoke to him as the only one in his world who knew exactly how he felt.

How many open doors are all around me —someone feels alone, someone waits to be inspired, someone is aching with rejection, someone is racked with guilt —just waiting for me to pay attention? — John Ortberg, *All the Places You'll Go . . . except When You Don't: God Has Placed before You an Open Door. What Will You Do?* (Carol Stream, IL: Tyndale, 2015).

8. Let's skip down to chapter 3. How would you summarize Jonah's story up to this point?

Jonah's closed door to God becomes God's open door to the sailors.

If Dr. Seuss were summarizing the story so far, it would go something like this:

> God says, "Go."
> Jonah says, "No."
> God says, "Blow."
> Jonah says, "So?"
> The captain says, "Bro."
> Jonah says, "Throw."
> The sailors say, "Whoa!"
> So they tossed Jonah in and he sank very low,
> But God had more places for Jonah to go.

John Ortberg, *All the Places You'll Go . . . except When You Don't: God Has Placed before You an Open Door. What Will You Do?* (Carol Stream, IL: Tyndale, 2015).

9. Jonah 3.3. How is the call different this time?

Isn't that good? There's no scolding or finger pointing. God simply repeats His original commission to Jonah, and gives him another chance.

The Bible doesn't tell us the location of the dry land where the fish deposited the prophet. Some scholars say it was somewhere on Israel's northern coast. But one thing is very clear: There were no delays, no foot-dragging in response to this second commission. The Bible says, "So Jonah arose and went to Nineveh, according to the word of the LORD."58 — Greg Laurie, *The Greatest Stories Ever Told, Volume Three* (Dana Point, CA: Kerygma Publishing—Allen David Books, 2011).

10. How do imagine Jonah felt as he walked toward Nineveh? What does it feel like to follow God?

You know, I imagine that however far Jonah had to walk to get to Nineveh, that was a peaceful journey. The prophet knew where God wanted him, knew he was (now) in the center of God's will, and knew that he was acting "according to the word of the LORD." No robbers or assassins would waylay him or block his progress; he was on the Lord's business. That's a great place to be. — Greg Laurie, *The Greatest Stories Ever Told, Volume Three* (Dana Point, CA: Kerygma Publishing—Allen David Books, 2011).

11. How did this feel differently than his walk to Joppa to take a boat to Tarshish?

Finding yourself in opposition to God's will can be very lonely. It also can lead to feelings of anxiety and fear. Don't let Satan and his forces confuse you. God has a way planned to lead you out of every dark situation, but it requires humility and trust in Him to be your Source of help. He will take your loneliness and use it as a tool to draw you closer to Himself.

If you have drifted in your spiritual devotion to the Lord, confess it to Him. Accept His love and forgiveness. Don't be fooled by Satan's lies. God can and will restore you fully and completely when you bring your sorrows and failures to Him. Even if you are struggling with certain feelings and have not yet given in to temptation, God can break apart the darkness that seeks to enslave you.

You have Someone who knows all about you, and He has chosen you as His beloved. Nothing comforts you more than knowing that God unconditionally loves and accepts you. — Charles F. Stanley, *Seeking His Face* (Nashville, TN: Thomas Nelson Publishers, 2002), 54.

12. Verse 4. What do you think of Jonah's message to Nineveh?

Jonah didn't give the Ninevites any good news in his message of doom, but God used it anyway. God touched their hearts in spite of the messenger, and they turned to faith in God and believed.

Why do I like Jonah so much? I think it's because he's so flawed—prejudiced, opinionated, and sometimes a little grumpy. I can relate to him! This is an authentic, flesh-and-blood guy. And even though he really didn't do what God had wanted him to do, in the end, he went ahead and obeyed. And God graciously used him anyway.

There are some men and women of God we may have a little difficulty relating to. But not old Jonah. He didn't really do anything great. He is more of a companion in our ineptness. Yet God worked through him, despite his shortcomings. God used him, even though he was a reluctant servant at times.

In the end, he obeyed God.

And God used Him to change his world. — Greg Laurie, *The Greatest Stories Ever Told, Volume Three* (Dana Point, CA: Kerygma Publishing—Allen David Books, 2011).

13. What is the lesson in this story for us?

When God tells you to do something, He wants you to do it. Now for Jonah, it was to go to a people he didn't want to go to. Maybe there's a call on your life to do a certain thing, but you don't want to do it. Maybe He has placed a particular neighbor, co-worker, or friend at school on your heart, and He wants you to go to that person and share the gospel. But you don't want to do it.

Perhaps this individual is quite "different" from you. Sometimes we only like to hang around with people who look like us, dress like us, think like us, and talk like us. But God wants us to leave our comfort zone and go to people that are a different age than us, a different race than us, a different socioeconomic group than us—or even people who are in a different nation from us. God has people on His heart who need to hear about new life in His Son, and we're His messengers, His ambassadors.

Jonah didn't want to obey that call. But reluctantly, he did. Notice his message: "Forty days and Nineveh will be overthrown!" Jonah knew very well about the mercy and grace of God, and he could have said, "This city is under judgment, but God is merciful and gracious!" He chose not to add that last part, because he didn't want them to repent. He still wanted the judgment of God to fall on them. So basically his message was, "Forty days and you're all gonna die!" And he might just as well have added, "To be quite honest, I'm not really that broken up about it. You guys deserve this. So prepare to die!"

That was his compassionate evangelistic message.

But in spite of this harsh, abbreviated sermon, God intervened and His Holy Spirit brought about a sense of conviction in that city, and the people repented and turned en masse to the Lord.

Unexpectedly, inexplicably, they believed, knew this message was true, and threw themselves on the mercy of God. This is probably the greatest revival in human history, because the population of Nineveh was something like 600,000 people at the time.

Jonah, however, was the right man at the right place at the right time...whether he was excited about it or wanted to be there or not.

I wonder if any of us are missing God's best for our lives at this point. Don't be afraid to yield yourself to the Lord. My life aspirations early on were to be a cartoonist or a pet store owner. But the Lord had a different plan in mind for me, and I've never regretted it. I can look back on things that I wanted to do, and realize that God always had something better in store for me.

Here's the best advice I can give you, no matter what your age, no matter what your circumstances. Never be afraid to commit an unknown future to a known God. If you're young, if you're middle-aged, of if you're 99 years old, just say, "Lord, I commit my life to You." Don't say, "Lord, please reveal Your plan to me and then I'll tell you whether I want to do it or not." No, how much better to say, "Lord, here's my life. I'm placing it in Your hands. I don't even to know what Your plan for me might be, but I trust You. Use me, Lord!"

Pray a prayer like that...and just watch what God will do. — Greg Laurie, *The Greatest Stories Ever Told, Volume Three* (Dana Point, CA: Kerygma Publishing—Allen David Books, 2011).

14. What do we learn about God from this story?

In Jonah's escapist disobedience the sailors in the ship prayed to the Lord and entered into a life of faith (Jon. 1:16). . . . In Jonah's angry obedience, the Ninevites were all saved (Jon. 3:10).

God works his purposes through who we actually are, our rash disobedience and our heartless obedience, and generously uses our lives as he finds us to do his work.

He does it in such a way that it is almost impossible for us to take credit for any of it, but also in such a way that somewhere along the way we gasp in surprised pleasure at the victories he accomplishes. — UNDER THE UNPREDICTABLE PLANT / Eugene H. Peterson, *God's Message for Each Day: Wisdom from the Word of God* (Nashville: Thomas Nelson, 2004).

15. Verse 10. We sometimes speak of our unchanging God. Does God change?

The third place where we read about God repenting is found in the Book of Jonah. I am devoting a whole lesson to this topic because the immutability of God is a topic of great importance. How can we trust God for tomorrow if we are afraid He will change?

In Jonah 3:10, God had sent Jonah to Nineveh, a mighty city, to preach a five-word (in Hebrew) sermon: "Yet forty days, and Nineveh shall be overthrown!" But the Bible tells us that the whole city turned to God: "Then God saw their works, that they turned from their evil way; and God relented from the disaster that He had said He would bring upon them, and He did not do it" (Jonah 3:10). Did God change? Did His words not carry the meaning that they appeared to? How do we reconcile this third apparent change of God's mind with Scripture?

From man's perspective, it appears that God changes. But when we see what God is doing from His perspective, we find the consistency that we expect in Him—and His Word. — David Jeremiah, *The Runaway Prophet: Jonah (Study Guide)* (Nashville, TN: Thomas Nelson Publishers, 1998), 107–108.

16. What changed as a result of Jonah's obedience?

The Bible says the people of Nineveh believed God (Jonah 3:5). The power of God's preached message changed a city of hundreds of thousands of people. How did that happen? It happened by the power of God. He empowered the preacher and gave him exactly the message to preach. When the people heard the Word of God, the Scripture says they believed God. Their belief and their faith in God began to change them. Here is the evidence of the power of God: The king sent a decree throughout the city saying,

> Let neither man nor beast, herd nor flock, taste anything;
> do not let them eat, or drink water. But let man and
> beast be covered with sackcloth, and cry mightily to God;
> yes, let every one turn from his evil way and from the

violence that is in his hands. Who can tell if God will turn and relent, and turn away from His fierce anger, so that we may not perish? (Jonah 3:7–9)

Everything about the city was changed because when the preaching of the Word of God was laid out in front of them in the power of the Holy Spirit, they heard and they believed. The Bible says that from the top to the bottom, from the greatest to the least, they all believed in God and were changed. That is why this goes down in history as perhaps the greatest awakening ever recorded in the annals of religion. — David Jeremiah, *The Runaway Prophet: Jonah (Study Guide)* (Nashville, TN: Thomas Nelson Publishers, 1998), 86.

17. Why did this change take place?

Please note, it was all of God. It was God-appointed prayer, a God-appointed preacher, and God-appointed preaching. A God-appointed place, a God-appointed period of time, and God-appointed power. When all those things come together, we should not be surprised to discover that a revival is taking place. God is anxious to do that today if we will preach the message He has given us to preach, and if we will go in the power of His Holy Spirit, but most of all, if we pray. — David Jeremiah, *The Runaway Prophet: Jonah (Study Guide)* (Nashville, TN: Thomas Nelson Publishers, 1998), 86.

18. Jonah returned to God and God's calling. What do we learn about returning to God from Jonah's example?

We don't use the word "backsliding" as much as we used to—but the reality is still with us: A seemingly sincere Christian begins to "slide backward" in their faith, returning to their old ways and acting as if Jesus no longer means anything to them.

Why does it happen? Sometimes their faith wasn't real; they had never committed their lives to Jesus Christ in the first place. The writer of Hebrews warned, "See to it, brothers, that none of you has a sinful, unbelieving heart that turns away from the living God (Hebrews 3:12).

But it also happens to believers—and when it does, Satan rejoices. Perhaps old habits overwhelm them; perhaps they cave in to the pressure of the crowd; perhaps temptation lures them into sin. Whatever the reason, a backsliding Christian compromises their faith and causes unbelievers to mock the Gospel.

The good news is that God loves even the backslider, and stands ready to forgive. Guard against sliding backward in your faith—but if you do, don't stay that way. Return to God—and He will return to you. — Billy Graham, *Wisdom for Each Day* (Nashville: Thomas Nelson, 2008).

19. What do you want to recall from today's conversation?

20. How can we support one another in prayer this week?

41620096R00037

Made in the USA
Lexington, KY
23 May 2015